Isn't It Lucky

Nona Moss

Presentation by *BookLeaf Publishing*

Web: www.bookleafpub.com

E-mail: info@bookleafpub.com

ISBN: 9789357441360

First edition 2023

Dedicated to my muse, the one person that inspires me! I love you, and I love you, and I love you.

ACKNOWLEDGEMENT

I could not write this book without the help of my muse. He inspires me without even knowing he is doing it! So I thank him profusely for giving me the words to put on these pages, and for making me believe in myself enough to try.

PREFACE

Every poem in this book describes a love so deep and so strong I cannot explain it any other way. Poetry to me is like music, as it feels the soul with emotions and energy you cannot get from any other source. There is no drug strong enough to alter your emotions the way those two things do.

Crazy

It's crazy how I feel like I'm finally okay
Then suddenly you're in my head
Like a train wreck, I can't look away
It's crazy how people ask how I am
And I say great, and wonderful, fantastic
Except even before I turn away, I am crying
And isn't it crazy, how it all comes rushing back
When I hear a song that reminds me of you
Drowning me with the weight of things I can't
forget
It's crazy because I know I am learning to live
Without you, without me, without a soul
Until the dreams wake me up, with the pain of
loss
It's crazy how the sound of your voice sets me
back
Back to I need you, and I can't live without you
And everything else just becomes irrelevant
It's crazy how I need you, and I need you to
leave
How I know better, but I pretend I can believe
you
How much loving someone can rip you apart
It's crazy how I feel like I can't live without you
How much I really don't want to live at all

How shattered I am from the greatest thing in
my life

I Am Addicted

I am addicted to
  The way you smile at me
The love in your eyes
  And the way you say I'm beautiful
I am addicted to
  The way you always smell sexy
At the end of the day
  And the taste of your sweat
I am addicted to
  The sound of your voice
Quietly in my ear
  Telling me that you love me
I am addicted to
  The way your skin feels
Melting against mine
  As you pull me into you
I am addicted to
  The way you make me feel
Like I am the world to you
  Like you are the world to me

Can We Talk

Can we talk about how much I love you
  How it takes my breath away
And I feel like I might be dying
  To be next to you again
And can we talk about how much I miss you
  How it's a physical pain inside
How just a single thought of you
  Leaves me needing you close to me
Can we talk about how much I need you
  How you're burned into my soul
The reality of our everything
  Is tattooed on my brain
And can we talk about how much I want you
  Burning against my skin
Your touch is the blood inside me
Boiling until I scream
  Can we talk about how much I love you
How you make me feel whole
  And how if I can't be with you
I would rather no longer be at all

Amazing

It's amazing how I get lost
In your touch, your smell, your eyes
And it makes me forget
Everything that's bad, and good
That ever mattered
And I am lost in the way you look at me
Like I am beautiful, perfect
Like I am the only woman in the world
And you're afraid I might disappear
With you, and into you
It's amazing how you consume me
Whenever we're together
How I'm so empty without you
Like a piece of me is missing
And I can't breathe
I don't know how you became my soul
How I've become so dependent
Consumed, with love
I'm so afraid of waking up
And it's a dream I can't get back
Of finding it's not real, you're not real
I'm not real

I Remember

I remember walking hand in hand
And dancing in isle two
The way you made me feel so beautiful
Even when I knew better
I remember falling asleep in your arms
A smile plastered to my face
And waking up in the morning
Thinking I must be dreaming
I remember the love in your eyes
And your touch, so perfect
I felt like I could go insane
I remember believing everything you told me
Because not believing would hurt
And telling myself I could fix you
Because there was no way I could let you go
I remember crying rivers, and lying to my
friends
And knowing I was going to die
If I had to watch you die
I remember walking away
And tearing my heart in two
Thinking I could be okay
And discovering how wrong I was
I remember every inch of you
You just can't be erased

And I will never get through a moment
Where I can't feel you under my skin

I Hope

I hope your heart skips a beat
When you see me across the room
And your breath catches in your chest
When I look into your eyes
I hope you can't sleep for hours
Because I'm consuming your thoughts
And you feel dizzy remembering
The last moments we had together
I hope that you feel empty
Whenever I'm not around
Like your soul has left your body
And you're missing a piece of yourself
I hope that your stomach hurts
With worry that I'm okay
And you know that if something's wrong
You'd kill to make it better
I hope that you stop breathing
On the last day of my life
And in that moment you're smiling
Knowing you don't have to live without me
I hope you always feel like this
And I hope it never goes away
Because this is how much I love you
And I want you to feel the same

I Want

I want to be the star
That leads you home at night
I want to be the wings
On which you take flight
I want to be the vision
Whenever you lose sight
I want to be the honor
For which you fight
I want to be the answer
You always get right
And when you're in the dark
I want to be your light

Isn't It Lucky

It's lucky I was able to find you
How it seemed it was meant to be
And the whole time I was searching
You were searching for me
It seems to be pretty crazy
The electricity when we touch
How our bodies melt together
How anyone can love this much
It's hard to imagine a life
Where you didn't have my heart
Because I feel like I can't breathe
Whenever we're apart
It's lucky I was able to find you
Because I also found me
Without you I feel irrelevant
To the person you inspire me to be
And isn't it lucky you love me
How our souls have become one
How we're living this dream together
Until we are old and done

You Are

A muse
  And music
    A shooting star
      Light through a tunnel, stretching far
A dream
  And hope
    A taste that's sweet
      The soulmate it took a lifetime to meet
The sun
  And moon
    The first day of Spring
      Butterflies in stomachs, only love can bring
An Angel
  A lover
    A one true love
      An answer to prayer, from God above
A soul
  And a life
    A brand new start
      Forever the one to have my heart

You Are (My Mistake)

The lightning
  And the thunder
    The calm after the storm

The ice
  And the wind
    The fire that keeps me warm

The rage
  And the tears
    My protector in the night

The fear
  And the dark
    The one who brings the light

The good
  And the bad
    Every breath I take

The beginning
  And the end
    Of every mistake I make

It's Sweet

It's sweet how when I'm around you
The world just disappears
And I feel like the whole planet
Is just you and me
And it's sweet how in that moment
I know I would do anything in my power
To make you feel loved
Like you make me feel loved
It's sweet how when you touch me
Every single part of me catches fire
And you're the only one who can put it out
How every breath I take
Seems to match every breath you take
And it's sweet how when I'm away from you
I feel like I am not whole
Like you took half of me
And left half of you
It's sweet when you whisper you love me
And my goosebumps get goosebumps
How when you look at me
I see what Heaven must look like
And it's sweet how connected we are
So we'll always be together
Even when we're apart
Our souls are always connected

Between the Lines

You are my world
　　My Darling, I love you so much
Drowning in darkness
　　Nothing could be more perfect to me
I feel so alone
　　My life, I've surrendered to you
I'm your captive
　　I'm exactly what you need me to be
I am totally dependent
　　Together, you've created a world of our own
And so afraid
　　I can't imagine one moment apart
We're bound together
　　I know you'll always hold me tight
Forever yours
　　You're breath is the beat of my heart
I'm a lost soul
　　I can never live without you
Until someday
　　You are my moon and sun
I break for you
　　My Darling, anything for you
And I'm nothing
　　As long as our hearts beat as one

*This is a 3-way poem. It can be read down the
left side, down the right side, or all together*

I Am

I am the one behind the one you think is me
  An image you only think you see
She has my face, she has my heart
  Side by side you couldn't tell us apart

I am the girl within the girl I'm expected to play
  Pushed back here, out of the way
I never seem to play the part right
  So I'm banished here, out of sight

I am the negative of the picture of perfect grace
  My dark mind clouds her pretty face
She's nothing more than someone's thought
  A doll with a string, waiting to be taught

I am the beast inside the beauty, you deny is real
  Catching the pain you won't allow her to feel
Floating in the tears, you can't see her cry
  Drowning in her sorrow, she won't let me die

Wreckage

It's no longer me you love
It's the memory of a dream
That flew out of sight
Caught by the wind of fate
And you were speeding way too fast
You couldn't clear the fog
As my grief fell like rain
It's no longer a dream to love
As your fog slowly lifts
And you face the wreckage of your past

I Miss You

It's insane how much I miss you
And I feel like I might die
Without the sound of your voice
For just a moment, or one second
I feel like I can't breathe
Like someone has taken my air
Like you took half of my soul
And left a broken heart
It's insane how much I need you
Just to get through each day
And how every beat of my heart
Becomes every breath you take
How I feel like I need to touch you
To believe you're not just a dream
And if I close my eyes too long
I'm terrified you'll disappear
It's insane how much I love you
Like no one has loved before
And how the whole reason I exist
Is to make sure that you know
It feels like you're so far away
And yet I feel you right here
Like even when I can't see you
I feel you whisper in my ear

Never Let You Go

I love the way you love me
I see it in your eyes
Just as deep as I love you
You complete my life
I love the way you hold me
Like I may disappear
Like the whole world will end
Without me here
I love the way you kiss me
Like you want to breathe me in
And you can't wait another second
To kiss me again
I love the way you need me
And how you let it show
The way we belong together
I'll never let you go

Without You and Me

I love you so much
It's a fire in my heart
Now this aching emptiness
Is tearing me apart
I gave you my soul
I gave you so much
Now my world is cold
I miss your touch
I need you right here
And I needed you to go
I thought I could live
But this world moves so slow
I love you so much
I just need you to see
Because it hurts so much
Without you and me
I gave you my soul
Now my world seems black
I can't take a breath
And I can't take it back
I need you right here
And I need you to stay
Because I'm sure I'll die
If you walk away

This Love

It's the feeling of sharing the same breath
After not seeing you for a while
Still feeling like we've always been
  It's the way your voice touches me
  And takes me places I never want to leave
  As long as you stay with me
It's the way a kiss is never just a kiss
No matter how long it's been
Our lips never forget home
  It's feeling like I can't breathe
  Because breathing might break the spell
  And you may just disappear
It's knowing I can't live
If I no longer have my soul
Without you
  It's love so deep, so real, so beautiful
  Touching is almost impossible
  The electricity pulsing through our skin
And like lightning
We burn into each other
To create something I'll die without

I Love You Too

I love you too, and it hurts
I love everything about you
You are so beautiful
Your face and your hands
And those amazing eyes
I love the muscles in your arms
When you hold yourself above me
I love your tattoo of Bonnie
And tracing it with my finger
I love the taste of your sweat
When we make love
And the way you smile at me
When you catch me staring at you
I love the sound of your voice
Telling me I'm beautiful
I love how you love me so much
That you can't stay away
Because I need you to know
I love you too

My Soul

You are my rock
You are my heart
You are the glue
When I fall apart
You are my hope
You are my dreams
You are my anchor
When nothing is as it seems
You are my laughter
You are my tears
You are my safe
When I have fears
You are my life
You are my all
You are my soul
So I don't fall

My Vow

It's crazy how I remember
The exact moment I fell in love
The instant that looked at you
And I just knew
It's impossible, the things we've been through
And it's taken a lot to bounce back
But even through the worst of times
I just knew
I'd sacrifice the world for you
There's nothing I wouldn't do
Because even now, after it all
I still know
You are everything to me
And I will show you
You hold my soul in your hands
And I will trust you
You are my destination
And I will follow you
You are my foundation
And I will love you intensely
Until we are old and done
And I promise you
Today and a lifetime
I love you, and I love you, and I love you

www.ingramcontent.com/pod-product-compliance
Lightning Source LLC
LaVergne TN
LVHW021341200726
843509LV00014B/2618